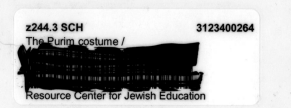

The
PURIM
COSTUME

Peninnah Schram

Illustrated by
Tammy L. Keiser

URJ Press • New York, New York

To my daughter Rebecca Schram Zafrany
who fills my life with blessing
with her joyous *n'shamah* and creativity.

—PS

To my family.

—TK

Library of Congress Cataloging-in-Publication Data

Schram, Peninnah.
The Purim costume / Peninnah Schram ;
illustrated by Tammy L. Keiser.
p. cm.
ISBN 0-8074-0874-3 (hardcover : alk. paper) 1. Purim––
Juvenile literature. I. Keiser, Tammy L. II. Title.
BM695.P8S37 2004
296.4'36--dc22
2004008503

I'm Queen Esther every year! I don't want to be Queen Esther again! And that's final!" Rebecca stamped her feet and put her hands on her hips.

"If you don't want to be Esther, then what costume do you want me to make for you? Purim is coming soon. The Jewish Museum is having a Purim festival with a Purim-spiel and a costume contest. If you decide today, I will still have time to make your costume," said her mother, trying to be patient.

"I don't know. Who should I be?" Rebecca replied petulantly.

"Well, if not Queen Esther, then how about one of her royal ladies?" asked her mother.

"No!" pouted Rebecca. "There are no royal ladies in the story!"

"Then how about being Mordecai? You can dress up like him, and no one would even guess that it's you. After all, Purim is a time for masquerade."

"No! No! No! I'm a girl," shouted Rebecca.

"Then how about one of the servants at the banquet, or the adviser who reads from the record book about Mordecai saving the king's life?" suggested her mother.

Rebecca shook her head.

"You don't like these suggestions either? Then how about being one of the objects in the story? The pillows at the banquet? Or a wine cup?"

"No! None of them are important enough. Besides, I don't want to be a *thing*!" replied Rebecca.

"Then how about being Vashti?"

"That's just dressing like a queen again," answered Rebecca with a dejected tone.

"Then be Vashti *after* she leaves the palace. Do you remember why the king took away her crown? Because he wanted her to come and dance in front of all his friends and show off her beauty. What a foolish and arrogant king he was! Vashti refused to be treated as just a decoration for his party. The king didn't like to be disobeyed, so he drove Queen Vashti out, and she began to wander. You could come dressed as Vashti in her bedraggled gown, looking like a beggar after years of wandering."

"But she wasn't important anymore when she stopped being a queen and became a beggar."

"Oh, but she was important. If it weren't for Vashti, there would be no story—and no saving of the Jewish people," her mother said with renewed excitement. "If Vashti had agreed to the king's request, he would not have commanded her to leave. It's only because she leaves that the king has to find a new queen. This new queen, a young Jewish woman named Esther, uses her wisdom and courage to help defeat the evil prime minister Haman and save the Jews. Do you see why Vashti is so important? Without Vashti, the story would have turned out very differently for the Jews."

Rebecca frowned. "All right, fine, make the costume if you really want to."

The Purim festival was about to begin.
The storyteller began to tell the story of Purim.

Good day to you, to those young and young at heart,
You're going to meet the characters, both foolish and smart,
It's a story of contests and a queen who saves the Jews,
We hope you have fun and that it will all of you amuse!
The place is Persia, the time is long ago and far away,
And now come with me as I take you to Shushan to start
*   our play!*

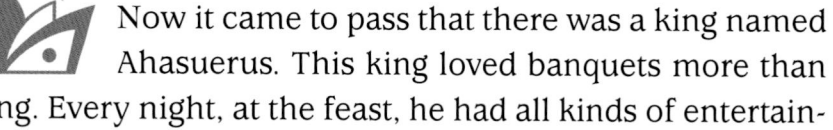

Now it came to pass that there was a king named Ahasuerus. This king loved banquets more than anything. Every night, at the feast, he had all kinds of entertainers. One night, at an especially lavish banquet, musicians played for the king and his courtiers. Suddenly, the king called out, "Command Vashti my queen to come here and to dance for us, but she must come wearing only her royal crown. Everyone must see her natural beauty!"

When Vashti heard what the king had requested of her, she refused to obey. "Wear only my crown? That I will not do," she said under her breath. Then turning to the courtier, she said aloud, "Tell the king that I will not come."

Now King Ahasuerus was a vain and foolish king. Afraid that all the wives of the kingdom would disobey their husbands if they found out that Vashti had refused his demand, he banished the queen from the kingdom. Vashti left that very night.

After some time, the king became lonely. His advisers said to him, "There are many lovely young women in this kingdom who would be happy to be your queen. Why not hold a contest to choose a new queen?"

This idea pleased the king, and immediately word went out that the king wanted all young maidens to appear before him. Among them was a beautiful and modest young woman named Esther. Mordecai, who was like a father to Esther, told her that she must go to the palace but not to reveal that she was Jewish. When the king saw Esther, he was filled with delight. "This is the one I choose," the king called out. Esther was crowned as the new queen of Persia.

Every day Mordecai came to visit her at the palace gates, bringing her news and homemade foods, and making sure that she was well. One day, as he was waiting for Esther, Mordecai overheard guards scheming to kill the king. Mordecai told Esther to tell the king. When the plot was uncovered, the guards were punished, and the incident was recorded in the king's book of records.

The prime minister was an evil man named Haman. Wherever he went, wearing his three-cornered hat, he demanded that everyone bow down to him. The only person who refused was Mordecai. "I bow down only to God," he proclaimed. This angered Haman greatly. Haman went to the king and complained, "Your Majesty, there is a people here in your kingdom who do not obey your laws and commands. They must be punished!"

King Ahasuerus, however, was too busy planning his banquets and entertainments. He turned to Haman, and with an impatient wave of his hand, he said, "Plan the punishment!"

Haman decided to kill not only Mordecai but all the Jews in the entire kingdom. He put some numbers into his hat and drew out the number fourteen. "That will be the day to kill the Jews, the fourteenth of Adar," he announced. He also ordered that special gallows be built on which he would hang Mordecai.

Mordecai ran to tell Esther that the Jewish people needed her help. He told her about Haman's evil scheme to kill every Jew.

"But how can I approach the king when he has not sent for me for thirty days? No one must approach the king without an invitation," said Esther desperately.

"You are wise, and only you can save the Jews, Esther. I am certain that you will know when you can tell the king about Haman's evil plan. Otherwise, not even you and your family will escape this harsh punishment. Perhaps this is the reason why you were chosen to become the queen," replied Mordecai.

"Mordecai, ask all the Jews to fast and pray for me for three days. I too will fast and think of a plan." After fasting for three days, Esther knew what she had to do. She decided to go to the king. As she entered the throne room, she hesitated, holding her breath. After what seemed like a very long time, yet was only seconds, the king raised the golden scepter, signaling for her to approach. Esther walked slowly to the king and greeted him. Then she said, "Oh King, I would like to invite you to a banquet tomorrow evening. And also your prime minister Haman."

The king happily accepted Esther's invitation. Haman also readily accepted.

Near the end of Esther's banquet, after feasting and drinking and entertainments, the king turned to Esther and asked, "What is your petition, my queen? What do you request? Even if it is half the kingdom, it will be done."

Esther replied, "Oh my king, I would like to invite you to a banquet again tomorrow evening. And your prime minister Haman also." Again the king was very pleased. And Haman was too.

That night, the king could not sleep. After much tossing and turning, he asked his adviser to bring the book of records and read about Mordecai saving the king's life. "What reward was given to this man?" asked the king.

"Nothing is recorded here," answered the adviser.

In the morning, the king called Haman and asked him, "What shall be done to the man whom the king delights to honor?"

"Whom could the king want to honor more than me?" Haman thought to himself. Then he said aloud, "Why, Your Majesty, dress this man in your royal robes, place your royal crown on his head, put him on your royal horse, and have your most exalted noble parade him through the town proclaiming, 'This is what is done to the deserving man the king delights to honor.'"

"So it shall be done! Make haste! See that all you have said is carried out, for I want to honor Mordecai. And you, Haman, my most exalted noble, shall lead the horse through the town."

That night, the king and Haman once again attended Esther's banquet. The king turned to Esther and asked, "What is your petition, my queen? What is your request? Even if it is half the kingdom, it will be done."

Esther said, "My king, if I have found favor in your sight, and if it please the king, let life be given to me and to my people. There is an evil man in your kingdom who has devised an evil plan to kill me and all the Jewish people, *my* people."

"Who is this person and where is he, that I may find him and punish him?" shouted the king.

And Esther replied, "The evil enemy of my people is here. It is Haman," she said.

King Ahasuerus stood up with great fury. "You, Haman, will hang on the gallows you built for Mordecai. But since it is too late to recall your order that the Jews be killed, I will give a proclamation that the Jews have the right to defend themselves."

These letters, sealed with the king's name, were sent with great haste and with special couriers to all the provinces from India to Ethiopia, 127 provinces. So it came to pass that the Jews fought bravely and won on the fourteenth day of the month of Adar. A day that was to be a day of dark and sadness turned into a day of light and gladness.

Chag Purim Samei-ach!

Musicians appeared on stage and led the audience in singing songs for Purim in Hebrew, English, Yiddish, and Ladino. The people clapped and sang, and the children danced.

Now it was time for the costume contest. "First, those dressed as King Ahasuerus," the judges called out. A few boys came to the stage, walked awkwardly across it, and the winner was announced. A huge wooden *grager* was presented as the prize.

Next came all the Hamans, the Mordecais, and, of course, the Queen Esthers. The Esther category had the most contestants, and the judges consulted together for a long time. Finally, three winners were picked. Then it was time for the last category, the most creative costume. In the end, both "The Gantze M'gillah" and "Gefilte Fish" were awarded prizes.

Suddenly Rebecca's voice cried out, "What about Vashti?"

The judges looked at each other. No one had ever come in a Vashti costume before. Hastily, the head judge announced, "Would all those who are dressed as Vashti come to the stage."

Only one person stood up and marched up to the stage—Rebecca. The head judge looked puzzled and asked her, "But Vashti was the queen. What does your ragged costume represent?"

Rebecca looked at the judges. "I'm Vashti after being thrown out of the palace, after years of wandering and being an outcast beggar."

"But why did you choose Vashti?"

"Because she's the most important person in the story. If Vashti had danced for the king as he had requested, Esther would not have been able to be the new queen. So we have to thank Vashti for helping to save the Jewish people too."

When they heard that, the judges all agreed that Rebecca had won the contest as Vashti. As Rebecca returned to her seat with her prize, a big wooden *grager*, she whispered to her mother, "This costume was a great idea, don't you think?" Her mother gave her a hug and said, "Good for you, Vashti."

That night at the *M'gillah* reading, Rebeccca spun that big wooden *grager* with all her might whenever Haman's name was read. And whenever Vashti's name was read, she held up a little flag that she had made with bells attached. Holding it high above her head, she waved it back and forth, joyfully thinking of Vashti, without whom Esther could not have saved the Jewish people.

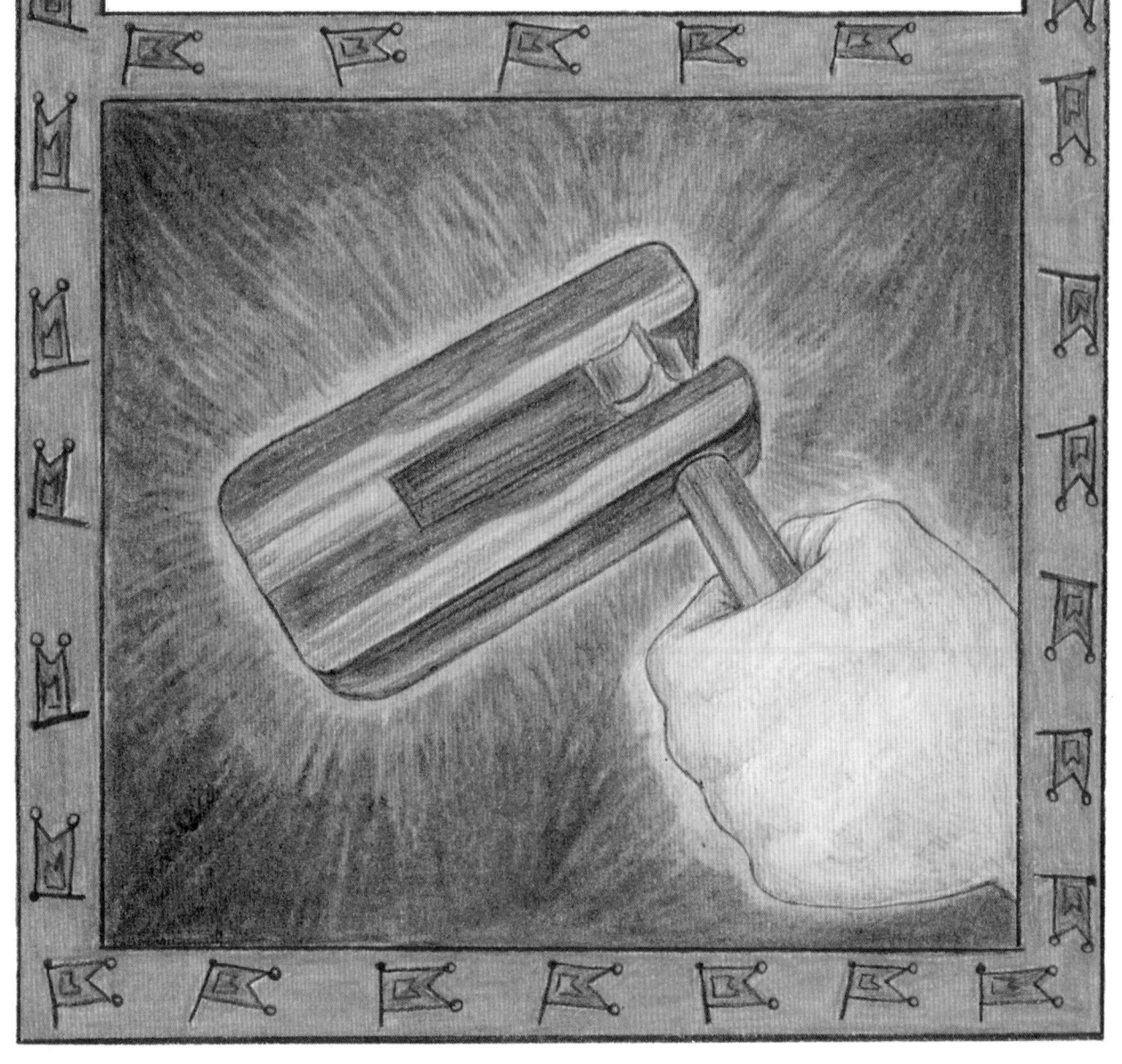

Glossary

Adar: The twelfth month of the Jewish year. Occurs in February or March.

Chag Purim Samei-ach: The greeting exchanged at Purim. *Chag* literally means "holiday." Purim is a festival synonymous with joy and celebration. Thus, it's a way of wishing someone a "joyous fun-filled holiday."

grager: Noisemaker for Purim used during the reading of the *M'gillah*, the Book of Esther. Whenever the name of Haman is pronounced during the reading of the story, there is a custom of drowning out the name of this villain. In some communities, people write Haman's name on the soles of their shoes and then stamp their feet to wipe out his name. Noise is encouraged in the synagogue only during a limited time after each mention of the name because there is an obligation to hear every word of the story.

hamantaschen: Traditional triangular-shaped pastry filled with poppy seeds or fruit. While it literally means "Haman's pockets," the triangle is like the shape of Haman's hat.

Hebrew: Biblical Hebrew is the sacred language of Jews everywhere. The Torah and the Book of Esther are written in Hebrew along with most of the other sacred literature. Modern Hebrew is the official language of Israel.

Ladino: This Judeo-Spanish language is the vernacular Jewish language of the Sephardim who were expelled from Spain in 1492. These Jews, in turn, brought it to the Middle East and other countries where they settled. It is a combination of Hebrew and Medieval Spanish.

M'gillah: The Book of Esther, or *M'gillah*, is the story of the events culminating in the celebration of Purim. It is in the form of a small scroll with only one roller and is unrolled as it is read.

Purim: This joyous holiday is retold in the Book of Esther, the *M'gillah*, which celebrates the deliverance of the Jews from Haman's plot to kill them through the courage of Queen Esther. Observed on the fourteenth of Adar, the Book of Esther is read in the evening and morning services in the synagogue. It is a time for costumes and controlled noise in the synagogue (see **grager**). On Purim, it is a custom to exchange gifts, especially of dried fruits, nuts, candies, and pastries (such as hamantaschen), called *shalach manot* (or *shalach manos* in Ashkenazi pronounciation), and to give money to the poor. It is also customary to have carnivals and stage Purim-spiels to create a sense of fun, masquerade, and participation, especially for the children.

Purim-spiel: A dramatic, sometimes improvisational play enacting the story of Purim. These theatrical performances began in Europe in the Middle Ages.

Yiddish: The vernacular Jewish language spoken by the Ashkenazic Jews of Eastern European countries. Yiddish draws on Hebrew, Medieval German, Slavic, and Romance languages.

Peninnah Schram, storyteller, author, and recording artist, is associate professor of speech and drama at Stern College of Yeshiva University. Her books include *The Chanukah Blessing* and *Jewish Stories One Generation Tells Another.* Her CD, *The Minstrel and the Storyteller: Stories and Songs of the Jewish People,* was recorded with singer/guitarist Gerard Edery. She is the founding director of the Jewish Storytelling Center at the 92nd Street Y in New York City, and has received the prestigious Covenant Award as well as the National Storytelling Network's 2003 Lifetime Achievement Award.

Tammy L. Keiser is a freelance artist specializing in illustrations, scenic design, and painting, as well as creating murals for homes and businesses. She has a B.A. in Fine Arts and an M.A. in Theatre Arts. She lives near Kansas City, Missouri, with her husband and two children. She has previously illustrated *The Perfect Prayer* and *A Year of Jewish Stories* for the URJ Press.